I CHANGED
MY MIND

JIMMY EVANS

I CHANGED MY MIND

JOURNEY TOWARD SPIRITUAL MATURITY

I Changed My Mind: Journey Toward Spiritual Maturity
Copyright ©2018 by Jimmy Evans

Content taken from sermons delivered by Jimmy Evans.

At Trinity Fellowship Church, Amarillo, Texas (fgc.org/watch-read/ messages):

March 31, 2013	I Changed My Mind About My Attitude
April 28, 2013	I Changed My Mind About Failure and Success

At Gateway Church, Southlake, Texas (gatewaypeople.com/watch/ message-archives/series):

May 4, 2013	I Changed My Mind About Worry and Anxiety
May 19, 2013	I Changed My Mind About Insecurity
May 26, 2013	I Changed My Mind About Fear

ISBN: 978-1-945529-32-0 paperback
ISBN: 978-1-945529-33-7 eBook
ISBN: 978-1-945529-34-4 Spanish

We hope you hear from the Holy Spirit and receive God's richest blessings from this book by Gateway Press. We want to provide the highest quality resources that take the messages, music, and media of Gateway Church to the world. For more information on other resources from Gateway Publishing, go to gatewaypublishing.com.

Gateway Press, an imprint of Gateway Publishing
700 Blessed Way
Southlake, Texas 76092
gatewaypublishing.com

18 19 20 21 22 — 7 6 5 4 3 2 1

Table of Contents

**PART 3 I Changed My Mind About Worry
and Anxiety**

PART 4 I Changed My Mind About Insecurity

PART 5 I Changed My Mind About Fear

Introduction

The Need for Change

Change happens whether we want it to or not; it's inevitable. Some people are creatures of habit; they want to do things the same way, every time. Others like to experience change. They want to "change things up," so that they can have more variety in their lives. Managing change has become a cottage industry. Several authors have written books about change—why we need it and how to manage it. A few business consultants have made careers discussing the topic.

We find that some things are easy to change. We might change everyday things, such as our hairstyles, clothes, or what we eat for lunch. However, I have discovered that the most important things are not our physical appearance, the clothes we wear, or the foods we eat. The important things are what we think and do.

God gave human beings the free will to think, act, and respond to the world around us. He has also shown us, as believers, how we should think and behave. The apostle Paul addressed this issue in Romans:

> I beseech you therefore, brethren, by the mercies of God, that you present your bodies a living sacrifice, holy, acceptable to God, which is your reasonable service. And do not be conformed to this world, but be transformed by the renewing of your mind, that you may prove what *is* that good and acceptable and perfect will of God (Romans 12:1–2).

The Greek word rendered as *conformed* means to fit into a fixed pattern, like a schematic. Paul uses this word to illustrate that we have become identical to something else. In this case, we have fit into the pattern of the world. If we conform to the world, then we will think and act the same way that the world does.

THE IMPORTANT
THINGS ARE WHAT WE
THINK AND DO.

Paul wants believers to know that God does not think it is acceptable for them to fit into the world's pattern. This pattern is not God's pattern. God created all things in the world, and His creation is "good;" however, Satan polluted the world through sin. God wants us to act better, above the world's standards. He wants us to *be transformed*. The Greek word translated as *transformed* is *metamorpoo*, from which we get the word *metamorphosis*. A metamorphosis is a complete change. For example, when a caterpillar enters a cocoon and emerges as a butterfly, it undergoes a metamorphosis. Those two stages of life represent both a complete end and a new beginning for the animal. It is still the same creature, but it looks and behaves quite differently. God wants His followers to have such a metamorphosis—a dramatic change in what we think and do.

How Does God Want Us to Change?

How does God want us to change? Paul says that God wants a transformation of our minds. It should not surprise us, then, that when a person accepts Christ, the new believer's life often becomes unrecognizable. Even people who previously knew the new believer now see a different person. As the butterfly is different from the caterpillar, so is the new believer different from the rest of the world. Of course, some people do not change immediately. Few have had an instantaneous experience like Paul's dramatic conversion on the road to Damascus (Acts 7:37–8:3, 1 Corinthians 15:3–8, Galatians 1:11–16). However, if we follow God's pattern, the eventual change will be noticeable and effective.

Paul characterizes this transformation as a *renewal* of the mind. Your mind is the part of your soul that activates or originates behavior, such as good works. However, because it is part of the soul, your mind is influenced by your emotions and other external forces. Our purpose as humans is to do God's will. Paul says that renewing our minds will enable us to know and, by extension, do *God's good, acceptable, and perfect will.*

As you *begin to* renew your mind, you will be able to understand the *good will* of God. As your mind *continues to be* renewed, you will then understand the *acceptable will* of God. Finally, when your mind *has* been renewed, you will understand the *perfect will* of God for your life. Understanding God's perfect will is the key element of spiritual maturity. You will be conformed to biblical ways of thinking, and, as a result, you will learn to live by the example of Christ with the help and power of the Holy Spirit.

How Do Believers Renew Their Minds?

This book is a brief journey into the process of renewing believers' minds. It may sound simple, almost silly even, but what our minds do is *think*. Consequently, we must understand what we need

UNDERSTANDING GOD'S
PERFECT WILL IS THE KEY
ELEMENT OF SPIRITUAL
MATURITY.

to learn to think about differently. This book is divided into five parts, and each part deals with one of the following concepts—attitude, success and failure, worry and anxiety, insecurity, and fear. Many things have influenced your thinking, so you will need to "change your mind." That is what I had to do, and I believe it is part of every believer's journey toward spiritual maturity.

MANY THINGS HAVE
INFLUENCED YOUR THINKING,
SO YOU WILL NEED TO
"CHANGE YOUR MIND."

Part 1

I Changed My Mind About My Attitude

Chapter One

Defining Attitude

The dictionary provides several definitions for *attitude*. The first definition is a settled way of thinking or feeling about someone or something, typically reflected in a person's behavior. We often think in certain patterns due to our upbringing, education, experiences, and emotions. Of all the topics that I will touch on in this book, attitude is the most pervasive and profound personal characteristic. In fact, changing your attitude is the precursor to changing your mind about anything. A change in attitude may have the greatest single effect on your behavior and success in life, except for salvation itself. The Bible records several examples of the importance of a change in

A CHANGE IN ATTITUDE MAY HAVE
THE GREATEST SINGLE EFFECT ON
YOUR BEHAVIOR AND SUCCESS IN
LIFE, EXCEPT FOR SALVATION ITSELF.

attitude. In the case of Jacob and Laban, the Lord took matters into His own hands to make up for Laban's negative change in attitude—

> Jacob heard that Laban's sons were saying, "Jacob has taken everything our father owned and has gained all this wealth from what belonged to our father." And Jacob noticed that Laban's attitude toward him was not what it had been.
>
> Then the Lord said to Jacob, "Go back to the land of your fathers and to your relatives, and I will be with you."
>
> So Jacob sent word to Rachel and Leah to come out to the fields where his flocks were. He said to them, "I see that your father's attitude toward me is not what it was before, but the God of my father has been with me. You know that I've worked for your father with all my strength, yet your father has cheated me by changing my wages ten times. However, God has not allowed him to harm me. If he said, 'The speckled ones will be your wages,' then all the flocks gave birth to speckled young; and if he said, 'The streaked ones will be your wages,'

then all the flocks bore streaked young. So God has taken away your father's livestock and has given them to me" (Genesis 31:1–9 NIV).

God intervened directly in another situation by changing the heart of a king:

For seven days they celebrated with joy the Festival of Unleavened Bread, because the Lord had filled them with joy by changing the attitude of the king of Assyria so that he assisted them in the work on the house of God, the God of Israel (Ezra 6:22 NIV).

The New Testament speaks about the need for a proper attitude and the change that occurs when it happens:

May the God who gives endurance and encouragement give you the same attitude of mind toward each other that Christ Jesus had, so that with one mind and one voice you may glorify the God and Father of our Lord Jesus Christ (Romans 15:5–6 NIV).

> Therefore, since Christ suffered in his body, arm
> yourselves also with the same attitude, because
> whoever suffers in the body is done with sin. As a
> result, they do not live the rest of their earthly lives
> for evil human desires, but rather for the will of
> God (1 Peter 4:1–2 NIV).

The apostle Peter shows the proper attitude
toward suffering, which Jesus modeled. Later in
the chapter, I will give a contemporary example
of this kind of attitude.

Consider this passage about Daniel's friends
and the fiery furnace:

> Then Nebuchadnezzar was furious with Shadrach,
> Meshach and Abednego, and his attitude toward
> them changed. He ordered the furnace heated
> seven times hotter than usual (Daniel 3:19 NIV).

The king's drastic action resulted from a change in
his attitude, which came about because of his anger.

The second definition of *attitude* is the position
of the body proper to or implying an action or
mental state, which is also called posture. When

I am preaching, I can generally read people's responses by the *attitudes* of their bodies or the expressions on their faces. Some English versions of the Bible, including the New King James Version, often translate attitude as "countenance." In the above passage from Daniel, it is translated as the "expression on his [Nebuchadnezzar's] face."

Another definition of *attitude* relates to the orientation of an aircraft relative to the direction of flight. For example, a plane may have a nose-up, nose-level, or nose-down attitude. Therefore, the attitude indicator of a plane— which I will talk about in more detail later in this book—is very important.

Attitudes tend to run in groups. Families and even businesses have their own attitudes. I guarantee that if you walk into any chain store across the nation, you can expect a certain attitude, depending on the store. I often fly on commercial airlines. I have come to expect that different airline companies have their own unique attitudes, both good and bad. Churches also have attitudes; again, they can be either good or bad. It is essential that we do not conform to other people's attitudes or ways of thinking, but instead conform to biblical ways of thinking so that we can know the perfect will of God.

As we study this concept, I encourage you to ask yourself this question: "After reading Romans 15:5, do I have a godly attitude or a worldly attitude?" Perhaps your attitude is different in one area of your life than it is in others.

Never underestimate the power of your attitude. In his book *The Winning Attitude,* John Maxwell says:

> It is the advance man of our true selves.
> Its roots are inward, but its fruit is
>   outward.
> It is our best friend, or our worst enemy.
> It is more honest and more consistent
>   than our words.
> It has an outward look based on past
>   experiences.
> It is the thing which draws people to us
>   or repels them.

It is never content until it is expressed.
It is the librarian of our past.
It is the speaker of our present.
It is the prophet of our future.[1]

As you look into your history to retrieve past events, your attitude acts as the librarian. You will either be grateful and think about the good things, or you will be ungrateful and think about the bad ones. You will be forgiving or bitter. Attitude is also the speaker of your present. You will always speak through your attitudes. Lastly, attitude is the prophet of your future. If you have a bad attitude, it will likely keep you from having the future that God wants you to have.

[1] John Maxwell, A Winning Attitude (Nashville: Thomas Nelson, 1993), 24.

Chapter Two

5 Truths About Attitudes

The following quote has been attributed to Thomas Jefferson: "Nothing can stop the man with a right mental attitude from achieving his goal. Nothing on earth can help the man with the wrong mental attitude." I believe this is true. Here are some other truths to consider as you think about your attitudes:

1. You Choose Your Attitudes

First, you choose your attitudes. Jewish psychiatrist Viktor Frankl was born in Austria in 1905. As an adult, Frankl had the opportunity to get a visa for the United States. He turned it down, though, and chose to stay in Vienna and care for his aging parents. In 1942, Frankl was transferred to a Nazi concentration camp. His wife, parents, brother, and sister were also forced into camps. By the end of the war, only Frankl and his sister had survived.

During the three years spent in four different camps, Frankl endured forced labor and witnessed his fellow prisoners dying of starvation and being murdered in the gas chambers. Despite all that, Frankl faced suffering with dignity. He chose to forgive and never to hate the Nazi soldiers or the civilians who had given up their Jewish neighbors. Surviving years of unspeakable treatment, Frankl's life became a monument to the human spirit amid suffering.

After his release in 1945, Frankl returned to Vienna to continue his medical practice and finish his writings about the meaning of life, which he had begun just prior to his arrest. I recommend his book, *Man's Search for Meaning*, which has sold over 12 million copies in 21 languages. In the book, Frankl describes this key tenet of his philosophy:

Most important, however, is the third avenue to meaning in life: even the helpless victim of a hopeless situation, facing a fate he cannot change, may rise above himself, may grow beyond himself, and by so doing change himself. He may turn a personal tragedy into a triumph .... If ... one cannot change his situation, he can still choose his attitude.[2]

Frankl became a lifelong proponent of his now well-accepted form of psychological treatment called *logotherapy*, which emphasizes the importance of an individual's search for meaning as superior to the search for power or possessions. Frankl continued teaching and writing until his death in 1997 at the age of 92.

2. Attitudes Are Not Caused by People or Circumstances

The second truth is derived from the first: people and circumstances do not cause attitudes.

[2] Viktor Frankl, *Man's Search for Meaning* (Boston: Beacon Press, 2006), 146–148.

We have been deceived if we think that a change in circumstances will give us a better attitude; it simply is not true. Biblical examples illustrate this truth. God created Adam and Eve as perfect people. He gave them perfect bodies and placed them in a perfect paradise. God lived with them. He walked with them in the garden. They had a perfect set of circumstances. God told them there was only one thing in all creation that they could not have, and it was a piece of fruit. Nevertheless, under the serpent's influence, they became ungrateful and rebellious; they took that fruit and ate it. You could not be in better circumstances than theirs were, but they had a bad attitude, which they chose with their own free wills.

During the worst times of his life, King David had a fabulous attitude, and in the best times, he had a bad one. When Saul pursued him, people turned against him, and his life was in danger, David wrote psalms. In those difficult seasons, he maintained a godly, humble, and faith-filled attitude. However, in the best times, David

WE HAVE BEEN DECEIVED IF
WE THINK THAT A CHANGE IN
CIRCUMSTANCES WILL GIVE US
A BETTER ATTITUDE; IT SIMPLY
IS NOT TRUE.

did things like sinning through an improper relationship with Bathsheba, followed by having Bathsheba's husband killed. Some of the worst things that David did were in the good times. His life illustrates that you cannot connect attitudes with people or circumstances.

The apostle Paul went to Philippi to preach the Good News about Jesus (Acts 16). The Philippian authorities captured him, beat him with rods, and threw him in prison. At midnight, though, Paul worshipped and praised God. Paul chose his attitude, and it clearly was not connected to his circumstances. You may be tempted to think, "My attitude is not right, but if my circumstances change, then it would get right." Don't believe that. It simply isn't true.

3. Happiness Is a Chosen Attitude

The third truth is that happiness is a chosen attitude rather than just a state of being. We choose happiness. Many of the greatest comedians came out of tragic circumstances.

Carol Burnett, a brilliant comedian, was the daughter of alcoholic parents. Her grandmother raised her. As a child, Carol had neither a bed nor a bedroom; instead, she slept on a couch. She studied under a dim light in the bathroom. Carol had none of the things that most people would consider requirements for a normal, happy childhood. Despite her circumstances, though, Carol decided to be happy and to make other people happy as well.

Happiness is a choice for all of us. Some people who experience miserable circumstances decide to make other people miserable. Others emerge from terrible backgrounds, yet they choose happiness amid and despite their circumstances.

Hugh Downs, a famed journalist and television personality, said, "A happy person is not a person in a certain set of circumstances, but rather a person with a certain set of attitudes." One of my favorite quotes on happiness comes from author Denis Waitley: "Happiness cannot be travelled to, owned, earned, worn, or consumed. Happiness is

SOME PEOPLE WHO EXPERIENCE
MISERABLE CIRCUMSTANCES DECIDE
TO MAKE OTHER PEOPLE MISERABLE.
OTHERS EMERGE FROM TERRIBLE
BACKGROUNDS, YET THEY CHOOSE
HAPPINESS AMID AND DESPITE
THEIR CIRCUMSTANCES.

the spiritual experience of living every minute with love, grace, and gratitude." You may believe that you are headed toward happiness but be sorely disappointed when you arrive at your destination.

Several years ago, one of our family members had a wedding in Hawaii, and we got a free trip to attend. That trip definitely increased my level of happiness. My son and I love to play golf, so we decided to play a course on the island of Lanai. Lanai is home to the Dole pineapple plantation as well as several marvelous resorts and golf courses. We chose to play at The Experience at Koele, a course right on the ocean with incredible, postcard-worthy views.

When we teed off on the first hole, some tiny black bugs began bothering us. We shooed them away, but sometimes they would return to sting us. As we reached the second and third holes, the bugs became even more of an annoyance. By the eighteenth hole, I started to wonder if hell was directly below us and this is where the demons came out. I was so miserable that I couldn't even think about golf. Later, I learned that these were pineapple bugs. They are definitely not on the postcards. On a postcard, you might think that happiness is in that golf course. And it is, except for those little demon bugs.

The devil will always tell you that you can find happiness. He will tell you that you can travel to it, consume it, or wear it. But I tell you that if you do not have happiness right now, then you will also not have it when those things come. You can choose happiness at any point in your life. Through a spiritual transformation, you can begin to live every moment with gratitude to God. It is an attitude, and it is your choice.

I will share another personal experience with golf. I have played since I was ten years old and a lot in college. When I married Karen, I golfed so much that it almost ruined my marriage. The better I played, the more I wanted to play to become even better. But when it threatened my relationship with my wife, I hung up my golf clubs. Our marriage was healed, though not just because I gave up golf. God healed our marriage because we turned to Him. Several years later, Karen told me that I was free to play golf again. At that time, the game became something of a spiritual experience for me—a sign of God's healing.

When I started playing again, I seemed to have lost my swing. I played terribly. I expected to become a good golfer again, but it just wasn't happening. Finally, after a particularly awful shot one day, I took my club and threw it as far as I could. Then, I started stomping up the fairway as my playing partners stared at me in dismay. I had this little conversation with myself on the way to pick up my golf club: "You are a preacher, and probably some people who go to your church live around this golf course and are watching you act like an idiot right now." Of course, the Holy Spirit prompted that conversation; it didn't come from me. I continued talking to myself: "You will never be a pro golfer; you may never be a good golfer again. And you are paying too much money to come out here, set a bad example, and be miserable. Now grow up, get over it, and play golf for fun—or stop playing!"

I picked up my golf club, put it in my bag, and I have had fun golfing ever since. If I play poorly, I have just as much fun as if I play well. I was miserable until I simply changed my mind about my attitude. You can be as miserable as you want to be, or you can be as happy as you choose to be.

4. God Rewards Good Attitudes and Disciplines Bad Ones

The fourth truth: God rewards good attitudes and disciplines bad ones. Good parents understand this truth. They don't wait until their child develops bad behaviors and habits; they discipline while the problem is still an attitude.

When he was about ten years old, my son Brent came home from school very upset one day. He said, "Dad, I got disciplined at school today for rolling my eyes. All I did was roll my eyes! I did

YOU CAN BE AS MISERABLE
AS YOU WANT TO BE,
OR YOU CAN BE AS HAPPY
AS YOU CHOOSE TO BE.

not do anything!" I replied, "I like that teacher, Brent. I am on her side." The teacher had told him to do something; Brent displayed a bad attitude, so she disciplined him. Good parents and good teachers don't wait until it becomes behavior; they immediately discipline poor attitudes.

God always loves us, of course, but like a good human parent, He will relate to us based on our attitudes. The Bible speaks about God's discipline of our attitudes:

> God resists the proud, but gives grace to the humble (James 4:6).

Is pride an attitude? Of course, it is. We can choose to be prideful or to be humble. In the verse above, James says that God gives grace to the humble, but He resists the proud. God still loves us when we are full of pride—we all deal with pride. However, when we are prideful, we are resisting God. God will discipline us. He loves us too much to not correct us when we are on the wrong path.

When we are humble, we open the door for Him to shower His graces on us, because He likes that attitude. He rewards that attitude. Humility is not the same thing as humiliation; instead, it is seeing ourselves correctly in God's light.

James says,

> Humble yourselves in the sight of the Lord and He will lift you up (James 4:10).

Sometimes all God is waiting for is a change in our attitudes so that He can bless us and give us the things we desire. He loves us, but He will deal with our attitudes. This is simply the truth and part of the way He grows us up. The author of Hebrews writes about God as our Father and the way that He disciplines:

> If you endure chastening, God deals with you as with sons; for what son is there whom a father does not chasten? But if you are without chastening, of which all have become partakers, then you are illegitimate and not sons. Furthermore, we have

HUMILITY IS NOT THE SAME
THING AS HUMILIATION;
INSTEAD, IT IS SEEING
OURSELVES CORRECTLY IN
GOD'S LIGHT.

had human fathers who corrected *us,* and we paid *them* respect. Shall we not much more readily be in subjection to the Father of spirits and live? For they indeed for a few days chastened *us* as seemed *best* to them, but He for *our* profit, that *we* may be partakers of His holiness. Now no chastening seems to be joyful for the present, but painful; nevertheless, afterward it yields the peaceable fruit of righteousness to those who have been trained by it.

Therefore strengthen the hands which hang down, and the feeble knees, and make straight paths for your feet, so that what is lame may not be dislocated, but rather be healed (Hebrews 12:7–13).

As your Father, God will discipline you because He loves you, just as any human father will do. So respect your heavenly Father even more than you would your earthly father. Everything He is doing, He is doing for your good—yes, even when He disciplines you. He is disciplining attitudes. This is why the author of Hebrews writes about "the hands which hang down, and the feeble knees." Do you remember the definition of attitude as body position? Or the rolling of your eyes?

To our grandkids, Karen and I are "Lolly" and "Pappy." Sometimes we babysit them. Not very many years ago, our son Brent and his wife Stephanie took a trip and left their two oldest children with us for five days. At the time our oldest grandson was one year old and his sister was five. (They now have another son). We dearly love them, of course; they are precious. Kate, our granddaughter, is so full of energy. One evening, Kate was enjoying the play area outside my office when Karen called to say it was time for dinner. I said, "Kate, it is time to clean up your toys, and we will go down for dinner." She responded, "Pappy I will pick them up later." Then I replied, "No, Kate, go ahead and pick them up; pick them up and we will go down for dinner." Thirty seconds earlier, this little girl was happily bouncing around, but as soon as I told her to do something she did not want to do ... Then came the "hands which hang down, and the feeble knees." I personally got to witness that scriptural posture with my granddaughter!

God deals with you as His children. You know discipline is over when you have learned the lesson. When Karen and I see that kind of response in our grandchildren, it reminds us that we adults can also misbehave sometimes. God wants us to recognize that attitude and the bad behavior it can lead to.

Therefore, God looks at us and says, "Children, I did not create you to be spectators; I created you to be warriors in My army and to rule and reign with Me. And because of that, I am going to grow you up to act like Me. I want you to be responsible, mature people, so that you can live victorious lives. I am going to deal with your attitudes." If you raise children, then you discipline them for their good, so that they will grow up and become responsible adults.

5. Attitudes Precede and Predict Your Future

The fifth truth about attitudes is that they precede and predict your future. You can know

GOOD ATTITUDES LEAD
TO SUCCESS, FAVOR, AND
PROMOTION; BAD ATTITUDES
PRECEDE AND PREDICT
A FUTURE OF FAILURE,
DISFAVOR, AND DEMOTION.

many things that will happen in your life because of your attitudes. Good attitudes lead to success, favor, and promotion; bad attitudes precede and predict a future of failure, disfavor, and demotion.

Do you remember the attitude indicator on an airplane? It is a simple instrument that lets you know when you are flying level, climbing, or dropping. The instrument displays a horizontal line, which represents the actual horizon. A dot above or below the line shows the plane's nose position. Marks on the instrument also indicate the position of the craft's wings, whether they are veering right or left. This vital instrument helps when the pilot cannot see due to clouds or darkness. Any attempt to fly without the attitude indicator, or the inability to interpret it, leaves the plane in danger. Without it, the pilot only has emotions and personal judgment to guide the plane. Emotions and personal judgment can't determine where the plane is headed, and the results will likely be disastrous. John F. Kennedy, Jr. died because he did not use this instrument correctly. As he was flying at night over the ocean, he lost his visual reference and flew straight into the water.

When you are going through difficulties, don't trust your emotions or someone else's opinions. God's Word is your attitude indicator. In the book of Psalms, David put his eyes on the Lord in the worst times. By his example, David shows us the attitudes that we should have when we are going through difficult times. When you cannot see outside or you are experiencing bad times, you can turn your eyes to the Word of God. It will predict whether you get out or not. It will help you pick the right attitude rather than the wrong one.

Abraham Lincoln is considered one of the most remarkable men in history and one of our greatest presidents. Learn from his life of deep faith ... a deep faith in God. Many people do not know of the difficult things that Lincoln experienced or how he emerged from them to become President of the United States.

Lincoln had a difficult childhood. He had only one year of formal education; otherwise, he educated himself. One sister died in childbirth, and only one of his four sons lived past the age of eighteen. Lincoln was in a very difficult marriage. He had two business failures. He lost six elections. Then Lincoln was eventually elected President of the United States in 1860.

I can imagine that during all those bad experiences, the devil came to him and said something like, "Lincoln, why don't you just get 'loser' tattooed on your forehead and lay down and die somewhere? What a pathetic loser you are." But I also know that the Holy Spirit was saying, "Just keeping acting like the President—you are going to be one someday!" In the midst of defeat and disappointment, Lincoln never gave up. He allowed God to determine his attitude rather than circumstances. Do not let your circumstances, other people, or life's disappointments cause you to have a nose-down attitude.

A negative, nose-down attitude will predict problems for your future. Stay nose-up. Put your faith in God and His Word. We often hear that attitude is more important than aptitude for success in life. Even if other people have more gifting, talent, intellect, or beauty, you can succeed over them with attitude. You may have heard that "a smooth sea never made a skilled sailor." In my office hangs a picture of a ship amid a raging sea. It reminds me that it is in the difficult times that I have always learned the most. And it is then that choosing the right attitude is the most important.

Chapter Three

7 Attitude Killers

Some ways of thinking will destroy your attitude. I call them "attitude killers." Ask yourself if you have ever fallen victim to one of these seven "killers."

1. False Expectations

False (or wrong) expectations will destroy your attitude. You may expect every person to treat you well. You may expect that your life will always be easy. Neither of those is true. You will always encounter people and issues that you have to navigate carefully.

2. "Comparing Up"

It is dangerous to compare yourself to other people who have some advantage that you don't. I call it "comparing up." If you drive into the parking lot and immediately begin to notice all the cars that are nicer than yours is, then you are "comparing up." That thought will kill your attitude if becomes your focus. Count the blessings that you do have—not what others possess.

3. Entitlement

If you begin to think, "Everybody owes me," then you have thoughts of entitlement. Take those thoughts captive and get over it! Nobody owes you anything.

4. Negativity

You have heard about people who see the proverbial glass half empty rather than half full. Faith in God removes this negativity. Faith allows me to see things in a positive light.

5. Pride

Proverbs says,
> Pride *goes* before destruction,
> And a haughty spirit before a fall.
> (Proverbs 16:18).
>
> God, however, gives grace to the humble
> (John 4:6).

6. Bitterness

God values forgiveness above almost all other virtues. Viktor Frankl could not have continued his remarkable life's work had he nursed bitterness and refused to forgive his enemies.

7. Self-pity

Self-pity may be the most dangerous of all attitude killers. When we feel sorry for ourselves, we begin to focus inwardly, which leaves no room for the Holy Spirit's power in us. When things are going badly, you might begin to feel sorry for yourself.

WHEN WE FEEL SORRY FOR
OURSELVES, WE BEGIN TO
FOCUS INWARDLY, WHICH
LEAVES NO ROOM FOR THE
HOLY SPIRIT'S POWER IN US.

Your boyfriend or girlfriend did not call you, you're having troubles at home, you can't pay your bills, or your boss is angry—all of these can bring on self-pity. If you are feeling sorry for yourself because of some circumstance, consider this story:

Jerry Long became paralyzed from the neck down because of a diving accident in high school. It rendered him a quadriplegic at the age of 17. Jerry learned to use a mouth stick to type and an intercom to communicate. He became a close friend and colleague of Viktor Frankl. Like Frankl, Jerry did not allow difficult circumstances to dictate his future. In 1990, Jerry earned a Doctorate in Clinical Psychology, and he went on to receive many awards, including the Michael Whiddon Award, the Viktor Frankl International Institute of Logotherapy Medallion of Responsibility, and the Viktor Frankl Award of the City of Vienna.[3]

---

[3] Viktor Frankl Institute. http://www.viktorfrankl.org/e/long_cv.html (accessed December 5, 2016).

After Victor Frankl passed away in 1997, Jerry shared the following memory about his friend:

Once, after speaking to a large audience, I was asked if I ever felt sad because I could no longer walk. I replied, "Professor Frankl can hardly see, I cannot walk at all, and many of you can hardly cope with life. What is crucial to remember is this—we don't need just our eyes, just our legs, or just our minds. All we need are the wings of our souls and together we can fly."

Chapter Four

7 Attitude Builders

As you avoid thought patterns that can destroy your attitude, you should adopt ways of thinking that will build it. I call these "attitude builders."

1. Gratitude

If you are thankful for what you have, you have a head start on a good attitude. Gratitude builds good attitude.

2. Faith

You can draw on the Lord's strength. Your faith in Him is critical to your attitude.

3. Humility

Humility is your ability to see yourself in the
light of who God is. It gives you perspective.

4. Graciousness

Graciousness means that you treat people
better than they deserve. Are you the kind of
person who always deals with people based on
how they treat you? Graciousness treats others
according to the "Golden Rule," regardless of the
way they act toward you.

5. Respect

Respect is deferential esteem given to others.
The Bible teaches us to respect our parents,
the elderly, people in authority, people of the
opposite sex, and people who are not like us.

6. Servanthood

Don't live for others to serve you; instead, serve
others the way that Jesus did. Jesus humbled

HUMILITY IS YOUR
ABILITY TO SEE
YOURSELF IN THE LIGHT
OF WHO GOD IS.

himself and took the form of a servant
(Philippians 2:8).

7. Contentment

You may want more, but until you get more—or
even if you don't—be thankful for what you have.
Contentment means that you do not need to have
more to be happy. Choose to be happy with what
you have right now.

Chapter Five

7 Reasons to Have a Good Attitude

Here are seven reasons why you should you have a good attitude:

1. It Is Christlike and a Good Witness

A good attitude is Christlike and serves as a witness to others of your faith in God and the difference that He has made in your life. You have it because you are, as Jesus said that He is, the light of the world. Because of Jesus, you are also a light and you witness to His light.

2. God Knows and Loves You and Has a Plan for You

God knows you, He loves you, and He has a good plan for your life. Jeremiah says:

> For I know the thoughts that I think toward you, says the Lord, thoughts of peace and not of evil, to give you a future and a hope (Jeremiah 29:11).

3. God Turns Bad Around for Good

God will take your mistakes and the bad things that have happened to you and turn them around for your good. The apostle Paul said:

> And we know that all things work together for good to those who love God, to those who are the called according to *His* purpose (Romans 8:28).

4. Nothing Is Impossible for God

God is bigger than your giants and mountains, and nothing is impossible for Him. Luke wrote:

But He said, "The things which are impossible with men are possible with God" (Luke 18:27).

5. Jesus Has Authority over the Enemy

Jesus defeated Satan, and He has also given you authority over the enemy and all his forces. Jesus said:

"Behold, I give you the authority to trample on serpents and scorpions, and over all the power of the enemy, and nothing shall by any means hurt you" (Luke 10:19).

6. Jesus Paid for Your Sins

Jesus died on the cross, paid for all your sins, and removed the curse of sin. Isaiah says:

Surely He has borne our griefs And carried our sorrows; Yet we esteemed Him stricken, Smitten by God, and afflicted. But He *was* wounded for our transgressions, *He was* bruised for our iniquities;

The chastisement for our peace *was* upon Him, And by His stripes we are healed (Isaiah 53:4–5).

7. Jesus Defeated Death and Hell

Jesus defeated death and hell. God raised Him from the dead, and now He sits at the right hand of the Father in heaven as our High Priest, Intercessor, and Advocate. The apostle Paul wrote:

Who *is* he who condemns? *It is* Christ who died, and furthermore is also risen, who is even at the right hand of God, who also makes intercession for us (Romans 8:34).

Today, Jesus sits in heaven as our Advocate. He is the one who loves you the most, controls the universe, and is ready to make intercession for you right now. He cares about everything in your life, and circumstances cannot change His love. He waits for you to adopt an attitude of faith, trust, and obedience.

Part 2

I Changed My Mind About Success and Failure

Chapter Six

7 Ways the World Defines Success

Failure is not the opposite of success, although the world often sees it this way. Failure is also not something that happens if you don't achieve success in a single area. In the Bible, success and failure have a broader application. We must relearn what success and failure mean from a biblical perspective.

What are the world's standards for success? Here are seven ways the world defines success:

1. Wealth

The world defines wealth (or financial prosperity) as having enough money to possess everything you desire. In fact, for many people, that is the only standard. Nothing else matters if they have money.

2. Popularity

Many people seek popularity through physical attractiveness, personality, talent, or some other means. They want others to know, accept, and like them. Some people sell their souls for popularity. In 1991, Wanda Holloway, the mother of a high school cheerleader in a Houston suburb, attempted to hire a hitman to kill one of her daughter's female classmates and the classmate's mother. That classmate had beaten out Wanda's daughter for a spot on the school's cheerleading squad. Wanda was actually willing to commit murder to ensure her daughter's and, in effect, her own popularity. Popularity became an idol for her, just as it has for many others.

3. Power and Influence

Some people seek power and influence through social, financial, or spiritual rank, authority, or ability. They believe it will give them the power to do as they please as well as represent and protect those about whom they care. Many people believe that if they achieve a certain rank, then they will have success.

4. Relational Happiness

Relational happiness is loving others and being loved in return. Everyone wants the kind of connection found in secure and meaningful relationships. In the world's definition, however, these relationships may take place outside of biblical moral standards.

5. Intellect and Education

Many people seek success through intellect and education. They define accomplishment through high intelligence and formal education in a desired field or at a particular school.

6. Giftedness

Some people see success as possessing special gifts, such as artistic ability, athletic prowess, musical talent, or any other area that fulfills their desires and makes them feel noticed and appreciated.

7. Strength and Security

Finally, some people believe they have achieved success when they are living in an environment of peace and safety, one that they have the ability to protect. Different cultures view this issue in various ways, but the feeling is universal.

King Solomon and Success

As you look at the world's seven standards of success, none of them are intrinsically bad or evil. In fact, we can use any of them righteously. However, you could have all seven of them and still be a complete failure. Notice that there is no spiritual definition among them. None of the seven standards address your spiritual life, because most of the world does not have a spiritual measure of success. Money, looks, power, and popularity—the world strives after all these things hoping to gain success. You can have them all and yet have no success in God's eyes because they are not His definition of success.

One of the best examples of how God views these seven standards of success can be seen in the life of King Solomon, the son of David and Bathsheba. Solomon became the wisest and most powerful man in the world. No person on earth will ever possess Solomon's wealth, and only Jesus surpasses Solomon's wisdom:

> So King Solomon surpassed all the kings of the earth in riches and wisdom (1 Kings 10:23).

MONEY, LOOKS, POWER, AND
POPULARITY—THE WORLD STRIVES
AFTER ALL THESE THINGS HOPING
TO GAIN SUCCESS. YOU CAN HAVE
THEM ALL AND YET HAVE NO
SUCCESS IN GOD'S EYES BECAUSE
THEY ARE NOT HIS DEFINITION
OF SUCCESS.

By the world's standards of success, Solomon had all seven. However, a problem soon arose:

But King Solomon loved many foreign women, as well as the daughter of Pharaoh: women of the Moabites, Ammonites, Edomites, Sidonians, *and* Hittites—from the nations of whom the Lord had said to the children of Israel, "You shall not intermarry with them, nor they with you. Surely they will turn away your hearts after their gods." Solomon clung to these in love. And he had seven hundred wives, princesses, and three hundred concubines; and his wives turned away his heart. For it was so, when Solomon was old, that his wives turned his heart after other gods; and his heart was not loyal to the Lord his God, as *was* the heart of his father David. For Solomon went after Ashtoreth the goddess of the Sidonians, and after Milcom the abomination of the Ammonites. Solomon did evil in the sight of the Lord, and did not fully follow the Lord, as *did* his father David. Then Solomon built a high place for Chemosh the abomination of Moab, on the hill that *is* east of Jerusalem, and for Molech the abomination of the people of Ammon. And he did likewise for all his foreign wives, who burned incense and sacrificed to their gods.

So the Lord became angry with Solomon, because his heart had turned from the Lord God of Israel, who had appeared to him twice, and had commanded him concerning this thing, that he should not go after other gods; but he did not keep what the Lord had commanded (1 Kings 11:1–10).

God appeared to Solomon on two occasions and made him the wisest man on the earth. Solomon later wrote the book of Proverbs. However, God had also given a command, not just to Solomon but to all the children of Israel: do not intermarry with unbelievers. Evidently, Solomon thought of himself as the exception. God told him not to marry foreign wives the way other kings of that time did. They would take foreign wives because potential enemies would then have grandchildren in the king's house; they would hesitate to attack. Foreign wives were an instrument of ongoing peace, but they were also a compromise.

So God told Solomon not to intermarry with foreigners. Nevertheless, the king didn't simply marry one or a few wives—Solomon married a thousand of them! Not only did he marry them, but the Bible says he clung to them in love. Clearly, Solomon changed his mind about God's command for marriage.

Then Solomon went even further. For every single wife, he built a monument and a place for her to worship her gods. Stop and consider that statement—the wealth that God had given to Solomon was used to build altars for these women's gods. Many of the Canaanite people worshipped Ashtoreth, a goddess of sex, fertility, and war. This worship included orgies, temple prostitution, and other sexual perversions. The Moabites and Ammonites bowed down to the gods Milcom, Chemosh, and Molech, all of which required child sacrifices. When the Bible says that Solomon built temples to those gods (referred to in Scripture as abominations), remember that their worship required offering babies as sacrifices, killing them on altars, and throwing them in fires. This method of sacrifice is the Old Testament's version of abortion. Since they did not have the medical technology to abort effectively in the womb, these people simply waited until the babies were born. Sometimes they even waited until a child turned two or three years old. If they did not like their children, they offered them up to Molech. The screams of dying children echoed daily from the valley east of Jerusalem where the temples stood. The anger of the Lord burned against Solomon, even though he possessed all seven of the world's standards of success.

Solomon was the most powerful man on earth. He had a thousand wives to love him. Solomon was the richest man on earth. He was incredibly educated and had intelligence beyond measure ... and on and on. Solomon met the seven worldly standards of success, yet the Lord's anger burned against him, and he died a failure. Unless we want to suffer the same fate, we must get the right definition of success.

Again, there is nothing wrong with these seven standards. All of us can use them in positive ways. I hold nothing against them, except this: I do not want to have all seven standards and yet have the anger of the Lord burn against me. I do not want to live my whole life pursuing those things, only to die, enter eternity, and discover that I failed trying to succeed.

Jesus Christ is our true example, and He did not meet many of those standards during His earthly ministry:

- For a short time during Jesus' ministry, He was popular; the crowds followed Him. However, the crowds also shouted for the Roman government to hang Him on a cross. Jesus never gained favor with the authorities, either.

- Jesus didn't have strength and security by the world's standards. The soldiers took Him, and He offered no resistance.

- Isaiah says that Jesus was nothing to look at, that we should gaze upon Him (Isaiah 53). We do not know if He was attractive at all.

- Jesus certainly never had financial wealth. He died penniless, and they buried Him in a borrowed grave.

In spite of all these "shortcomings," our Savior was the most successful person who ever lived. No one will ever have the success of our Lord Jesus Christ. In the world's eyes, however, He was a failure by several of these standards. King Solomon met all seven and died a failure. Jesus had very few and died an unparalleled success. The comparison between these two men should cause you to question everything you think about success and the way you live.

Chapter Seven

5 Results of the Wrong Standards for Success

What will happen if you have the wrong standards for success?

1. A Flawed Sense of Success or Failure

The wrong standards for success will give you a false sense of success or failure. Some people consider themselves successful, but in God's eyes they're not. On the other hand, you may think of yourself as a failure when, in fact, you are highly successful (even if you don't even realize it). You have a flawed sense of success or failure because you use the wrong standards to judge them.

2. Wrong Parenting and Modeling

Another result of having the wrong standards for success is that you will parent and model the wrong things to your children. After all, they depend on your example.

When I was in business, a man came up to me and offered me lots of money to work for him. I was a good salesman. I come from a family of salespeople, and we just instinctively know how to sell. This man knew my talent and offered a huge salary. At the time, Karen and I were very involved in our church. I facilitated a lifegroup, and I taught Sunday school. Karen also had a lifegroup and worked in the nursery. Then this man said, "If you come to work for me, you are going to have to work nights and weekends."

He was sitting in my living room, and Karen was there as well. I looked at him and said, "I won't work nights and weekends. We have our church, we have our lifegroups, and that is just an inviolable part of our lives." And then the man mocked me. He laughed at me right there in my living room. He told me that I was a fool for not giving up my lifegroup and church to make money.

That incident happened over thirty years ago, and, today, I thank God that I told him "no." He was wrong about success. I will not sell my soul for money, and I've taught my children not to sell their souls either.

Some parents have adopted the wrong standards of success. They teach their children to be busy with school, with sports, with their friends; and then God comes last. When you raise your children that way, they grow up the same as adults. They put money first. Friends come first. Popularity is first. All those things come first. Then, if they can fit God in, He comes somewhere down the list. We taught our children that God is first—period! God and the church are primary. We will not sacrifice Him for anything.

Remember, those seven standards of worldly success do not contain a spiritual element, so it is no wonder that if we parent based on worldly values, our children will grow up thinking of success in those terms. We must raise our children to love God first, and then everything else comes after that. If your children love God first, they will succeed in life.

3. Wrong Decision-Making

If you have the wrong standards for success, it will result in wrong decision-making. Sometimes when I speak to young people, I love the saying, "Choose a career that fills your heart first and your pocketbook second." The following true story illustrates just that.

My brother worked as the administrator of a psychiatric hospital in Houston, Texas. The hospital admitted a man in great mental distress; he seemed to have lost his mind. They discovered that he had just graduated from dental school. His grandfather, father, uncles, and brothers all became dentists, so by default, he became one too. The family knew it was a profitable profession.

Suddenly, when he graduated from dental school, he simply lost his mind. As the hospital

IF YOUR CHILDREN
LOVE GOD FIRST, THEY
WILL SUCCEED IN LIFE.

was treating him, he said, "I hate putting my hands in another person's mouth. I hate everything about dentistry. And in dental school, I just kind of blocked it out. But the day I graduated, I realized I have got to start putting my hands in people's mouths for the rest of my life." Then he said, "I can't take it. I do not want to do that for a living just because my granddaddy did it, my daddy, or anybody else. I want to do what I want to do for a living, because God called me to do it."

Some of the most important and valuable people in society do not get paid enough and never will—police officers, firefighters, teachers, and other professions like that. Military people do what they do because they have a calling to do it. They are sacrificing wealth for the sake of doing what they love. I respect those people. If you make a lot of money, then good for you. God may have called you to do that. However, I am saying that you should not choose a career just for the money you will make. That is what the world tells you to do. But what does God say?

4. Lack of Inner Fulfillment

A lack of inner fulfillment is another problem with having the wrong standards of success. This experience happens so often in people's lives. You may do everything the world tells you to do to succeed, but something deep inside is simply missing. You are on the wrong path.

5. Not Accomplishing God's Best

Using the wrong standards of success means that you will not accomplish God's best for your life. King Solomon died a failure; he did not finish the race well. Why did this happen? Remember, the apostle Paul tells us not to be conformed to this world, but to be transformed (Romans 12:2). At first, Solomon was transformed. The most successful man in the world, he wrote the book of Proverbs to expound on morals, speech, and money—everything that's important in life. He was able to write Proverbs because God had transformed his mind to think like God. Later, however, Solomon's foreign wives conformed him to a worldly way of thinking. If you want true success, then you must follow God's definition and not the world's.

Chapter Eight

God's 3 Essential Standards for Success

God defines success by three essential standards. The apostle Matthew recorded three parables in Matthew chapter 25, which show us what success really looks like in God's eyes. At the end of Matthew chapter 24, the disciples asked Jesus when He would come again. He told them about the signs to look for, how to prepare, and how to behave, so that they could be ready when He comes. However, Jesus also said that they would not know the exact time, implying that they should always be prepared.

1. Parable of the Ten Virgins: A Personal Relationship with Jesus

Then Jesus began to teach in parables:

Then the kingdom of heaven shall be likened to ten virgins who took their lamps and went out to meet the bridegroom. Now five of them were wise, and five *were* foolish. Those who *were* foolish took their lamps and took no oil with them, but the wise took oil in their vessels with their lamps. But while the bridegroom was delayed, they all slumbered and slept.

And at midnight a cry was *heard:* "Behold, the bridegroom is coming; go out to meet him!" Then all those virgins arose and trimmed their lamps. And the foolish said to the wise, "Give us *some* of your oil, for our lamps are going out." But the wise answered, saying, "*No,* lest there should not be enough for us and you; but go rather to those who sell, and buy for yourselves." And while they went to buy, the bridegroom came, and those who were ready went in with him to the wedding; and the door was shut.

Afterward the other virgins came also, saying,

"Lord, Lord, open to us!" But he answered and said,
"Assuredly, I say to you, I do not know you."

Watch therefore, for you know neither the day
nor the hour in which the Son of Man is coming
(Matthew 25:1–13).

The bridegroom in the story (who represents
Jesus) answered the foolish virgins, "I do not
know you."

The first and most important biblical standard
of success is a personal relationship with Jesus.
The story of the rich man and the beggar named
Lazarus (Luke 16:19–31) emphasizes this same
principle. Lazarus waited outside the rich man's
door. He had sores on his feet, and the dogs
came to lick his sores. The rich man gave no
comfort to him.

One day, both men died. Lazarus was carried to
Abraham's bosom (paradise), while the rich man
went to torment in Hades. The rich man peered
over the divide to Abraham and asked him simply
to have Lazarus dip his finger in some water and

touch the rich man's tongue to help quench the flames.[4] Abraham replied that this was impossible because there was a great gulf, a great chasm, that stood between them. No one could pass across it, and it would endure forever.

Jesus is the first biblical standard for success, but you only have the option to follow Him while you still live. If you know Jesus, you will go to heaven—if you don't, you will go to hell. The amount of money you have does not apply. The rich man no longer had any money when he went to hell; he was broke. But the poor man, Lazarus, had the riches of heaven; everything had changed.

Notice two additional elements in the parable of the ten virgins. First, Jesus told about five wise and five foolish virgins; the proportion of the two groups is important. The bridegroom told the five foolish ones that he never knew them. I believe that these five represent half of those who profess that they are Christians but do not

---

[4] In this story, the beggar had been seeking just "crumbs" from the rich man's table.

really know Jesus. They simply want to be part of the wedding party. Perhaps their parents were believers, but they don't really know Jesus for themselves. Through His death, Jesus offers a personal relationship, not simply an offer to join in an exercise that appears religious.

Second, the oil in the story represents time. You can borrow money, but you cannot borrow time. The wise virgins used their oil to prepare to know the bridegroom. They did not wait until the last minute. Remember, Jesus had just told His disciples that they would not know the time of His coming. The foolish virgins wasted their time. So when the bridegroom (Jesus) eventually came, they were not ready. They could not share the personal relationship like the wise virgins had with the bridegroom. They had time to prepare, but they failed.

It doesn't matter if your parents were Christians—it doesn't make you a Christian. It doesn't matter if you went to a church building 1,000 times. Only one question matters: "Do you

THROUGH HIS DEATH,
JESUS OFFERS A PERSONAL
RELATIONSHIP, NOT SIMPLY
AN OFFER TO JOIN IN AN
EXERCISE THAT APPEARS
RELIGIOUS.

know Jesus?" It is not: "Do you just know about Him?" Do you have a personal relationship with Him? That is the first biblical standard of success, and it is not one shared by most of the world. Don't let anything get in the way of Jesus Christ in your life, and do not put Him off until it is too late!

2. Parable of the Talents: Living for God and Not Only Yourself

The second story Jesus tells is the parable of the talents. The focus of the story is really about the actions of the three servants, or stewards, concerning their master's funds:

For *the kingdom of heaven is* like a man traveling to a far country, *who* called his own servants and delivered his goods to them. And to one he gave five talents, to another two, and to another one, to each according to his own ability; and immediately he went on a journey. Then he who had received the five talents went and traded with them, and made another five talents. And likewise he who *had received* two gained two more also. But he who had received one went and dug in the ground, and hid his lord's money. After a long time the lord of those servants came and settled accounts with them.

So he who had received five talents came and brought five other talents, saying, "Lord, you delivered to me five talents; look, I have gained five more talents besides them." His lord said to him, "Well *done,* good and faithful servant; you were faithful over a few things, I will make you ruler over many things. Enter into the joy of your lord." He also who had received two talents came and said, "Lord, you delivered to me two talents; look, I have gained two more talents besides them." His lord said to him, "Well *done,* good and faithful servant; you have been faithful over a few things, I will make you ruler over many things. Enter into the joy of your lord."

Then he who had received the one talent came and said, "Lord, I knew you to be a hard man, reaping where you have not sown, and gathering where you have not scattered seed. And I was afraid, and went and hid your talent in the ground. Look, *there* you have *what is* yours."

But his lord answered and said to him, "You wicked and lazy servant, you knew that I reap where I have not sown, and gather where I have not scattered seed. So you ought to have deposited my money with the bankers, and at my coming I would have received back my own with interest. Therefore take the talent from him, and give *it* to him who has ten talents.

"For to everyone who has, more will be given, and he will have abundance; but from him who does not have, even what he has will be taken away. And cast the unprofitable servant into the outer darkness. There will be weeping and gnashing of teeth" (Matthew 25:14–30).

The master went away on a long journey. He entrusted to one steward five talents, which is equivalent to approximately $1.5 million today. To another, he entrusted two talents, approximately $600 thousand now. Finally, he gave the last servant one talent (around $300 thousand). Eventually, the master returned. The servant with five talents had invested them and returned five more. The servant with two had also invested, and he returned two more. However, the servant who received one talent had hidden it in the ground because he feared his master.

The focus of this story is not money, or at least it's not primarily money. The talents represent the gifts or blessings that God gives you to further His kingdom. You don't have to do works to go to heaven. But it is clear that your Master, like the one in this parable, will hold you accountable for how you use those gifts. Did you use them for the glory of God and Christ's kingdom? Did you invest them in bringing others to know Him? Or did you sit on the side and watch? Did you work to accumulate wealth and worldly success? Or did you gather people, God's most precious asset, to share in His kingdom's glory? God wants you to show a profit, and that profit is people. God values human souls more than anything else.

GOD WANTS YOU TO SHOW
A PROFIT, AND THAT PROFIT
IS PEOPLE. GOD VALUES
HUMAN SOULS MORE THAN
ANYTHING ELSE.

I also want you to notice that the master rewards both the servant with five talents and the one with two. Whether a servant directs cars in the church parking lot, takes care of children in the nursery, or preaches in front of 30,000 people every week, God values in equal measure the return that they make with their respective talents. What impact is your life having on other lives? Are you giving God a return on His investment in you, or are you lost in your own limited story?

The second standard for success is this: are you living for God or only for yourself? There is a kingdom that we have the privilege to serve. There is a world of lost and hurting people that we get to reach. When we get to heaven, we will receive the eternal reward for what we have allowed God to do through us in this life. That is success—living your life for God.

3. Parable of the Sheep and the Goats: Treat Others with Compassion

Jesus tells a third parable, this one about the sheep and the goats.

When the Son of Man comes in His glory, and all the holy angels with Him, then He will sit on the throne of His glory. All the nations will be gathered before Him, and He will separate them one from another, as a shepherd divides *his* sheep from the goats. And He will set the sheep on His right hand, but the goats on the left. Then the King will say to those on His right hand, "Come, you blessed of My Father, inherit the kingdom prepared for you from the foundation of the world: for I was hungry and you gave Me food; I was thirsty and you gave Me drink; I was a stranger and you took Me in; I *was* naked and you clothed Me; I was sick and you visited Me; I was in prison and you came to Me."

Then the righteous will answer Him, saying, "Lord, when did we see You hungry and feed *You,* or thirsty and give *You* drink? When did we see You a stranger and take *You* in, or naked and clothe *You?* Or when did we see You sick, or in prison, and come to You?" And the King will answer and say to them, "Assuredly, I say to you, inasmuch as you did *it* to one of the least of these My brethren, you did *it* to Me."

Then He will also say to those on the left hand, "Depart from Me, you cursed, into the everlasting fire prepared for the devil and his angels: for I was hungry and you gave Me no food; I was thirsty and you gave Me no drink; I was a stranger and you did not take Me in, naked and you did not clothe Me, sick and in prison and you did not visit Me."

Then they also will answer Him, saying, "Lord, when did we see You hungry or thirsty or a stranger or naked or sick or in prison, and did not minister to You?" Then He will answer them, saying, "Assuredly, I say to you, inasmuch as you did not do *it* to one of the least of these, you did not do *it* to Me." And these will go away into everlasting punishment, but the righteous into eternal life (Matthew 25:31–46).

The Son of Man comes in His glory, along with holy angels, and sits on His throne. He separates the flock and sets the sheep on His right and the goats on His left. The sheep—the righteous—receive praise for feeding, clothing, and caring for Him; when they did it for the least of the brethren, they did it for Jesus. Conversely, those on the left—the unrighteous—are punished for failing to serve others.

According to Jesus, the third biblical standard for success is treating others with compassion and respect, regardless of what they have done or can do for you. The world's standard of accumulating wealth and self-promotion only makes you selfish. Many successful people in the world are hard-hearted and self-centered. We see that behavior far too often. When you know Jesus, He guarantees eternal life for you. But if you really know and obey Him, you will serve a higher purpose than yourself and will treat others with love and compassion.

Heaven's Reward

Notice that in all three parables everyone looks the same until the end. The stewards go about their business, the virgins all look fine, and the sheep and goats remain together. But in the end, God's standard lasts for eternity, and He judges and separates. He is a just God. It doesn't matter how much money you make, what you look like, how smart or talented you are, or what status you hold. If you know Jesus, live for Him, and treat others with love, you will have everything you need for success on earth—and in heaven. All things will be fully revealed and rewarded.

Part 3

I Changed My Mind About Worry and Anxiety

Chapter Nine

The Problem of Worry and Anxiety

Anxiety is the state of unease or nervousness about an event, person, or problem that you cannot control. Since you can't control it, you feel anxious about it. Worry is mentally dwelling on a difficulty or trouble. It is often a chronic, ongoing concern. Worry is usually the milder of the two emotions and related to something specific. Anxiety and worry are related to each other, but they are also related to fear, which is usually a higher-level emotion. I will address fear at length later in the book.

The apostle Paul tells the Philippian church not to be anxious (Philippians 4:6). However, in the United States alone, over 40 million adults have been diagnosed with anxiety disorders[5]. In addition to interfering with day-to-day functioning, psychological distress has also been shown to reduce life expectancy[6]. In Matthew's gospel, Jesus said not to worry about your life, or what you will eat, drink, or wear (Matthew 6:25). Then He said not to worry about tomorrow, for tomorrow has its own set of troubles (Matthew 6:34).

I grew up with a great deal of worry and anxiety. I tried hard not to present myself that way to others, but still I had a great deal of anxiety. It caused skin problems, like eczema, and other physical problems. At the age of 20, I consulted a doctor about my skin problems. He examined me and then left the room. Soon, a nurse entered. I expected to get my prescription and go back home. However, she came in, put a cassette into a cassette player, pushed the

[5] Anxiety and Depression Association of America. "Facts and Statistics." ADAA.org. https://www.adaa.org/about-adaa /press-room/facts-statistics (Accessed March 30, 2017).
[6] Tom C. Russ et al., *BMJ* 2012;345:e4933

play button, and left the room. The tape was about worry. Frankly, I was angry at the time. I didn't come to the doctor to get a sermon! I just wanted medicine. But what I had was more than a physical problem—it was an emotional problem that became a physical problem.

I also had relationship difficulties, problems with pleasing people, and struggles with control. I got saved, which helped some at first, as did the baptism in the Holy Spirit. Then, however, I entered full-time ministry. Karen and I were members of Trinity Fellowship in Amarillo, Texas. I first joined the staff as a marriage counselor, but only 10 months later, in June 1983, I became the senior pastor. A year earlier, I had been in the home appliance business. I had never conducted a wedding or a funeral. I had never led a staff. I had only prepared a couple of sermons.

When I entered the ministry, I felt anxious about everything: job failure, financial security, rejection—many things. The constant worry and anxiety contributed to problems with my relationships and my emotions, especially in my marriage and family. I was a distracted husband and parent.

But I know that the root of all worry and anxiety is the same—it is an *orphan spirit*. God absolutely loves to be a Daddy. The context of Jesus' instruction not to worry began with the assertion that God cares for us as a Father. The reason that I grew up with so much worry and anxiety was that I didn't know I had a Father, someone who was taking care of me. Even though I prayed as a pastor and had a relationship with God, I didn't understand just how much He loves being my Father.

I have two children and five grandchildren. I love being a father and a grandfather—a Pappy— even more. When my children or grandchildren ask me to do something, it is one of the greatest joys in my life. Still, I am evil compared to my heavenly Father. God adores you. He knows every hair on your head and everything you're facing. He loves being our Daddy through every circumstance. The root issue of all chronic worry and anxiety is this orphan spirit and not understanding how much God loves us.

One night, I had a dream that showed me my disconnectedness from God. I usually just have meaningless dreams. I had never had a spiritual dream until then. That night, Karen and I were watching TV, and she turned on a Hallmark movie, which some men enjoy but mostly women watch. I took that as my cue to retire to my office and watch something I would enjoy. I enjoy watching Chinese war movies. Yes, I really do— those English-subtitled ones, which are actually made in China. I turned on a movie called *War of the Arrows*. Its theme is fear and worry. It depicts a dissident family with a ten-year-old boy, who watches the government kill his family. Then he escapes and spends the rest of his life becoming a warrior and dealing with his fears.

Right after watching that movie, I fell sleep and had an all-night, full-color, 3D dream. In it, there were several hundred of my favorite people—my

THE ROOT ISSUE OF
ALL CHRONIC WORRY
AND ANXIETY IS THIS
ORPHAN SPIRIT AND NOT
UNDERSTANDING HOW MUCH
GOD LOVES US.

family, church family, and friends. My mom and dad were there, looking about 35 years old. (In reality, they were both in their mid-80s at the time). Everyone was celebrating and having a great time. Just then, I glanced over and saw Osama bin Laden sitting at a table, handcuffed and right in the middle of this group. We all knew that he was there to be executed. Everyone, except bin Laden and me, joined in the party. In the dream, I worried all night long. I thought Al Qaida terrorists probably surrounded us. Eventually, I searched for and located a gun to kill bin Laden. I found some security guards and asked them to help me take bin Laden out back to a shed to kill him. As I put the gun up to his head, I turned to the people there and said, "Don't tell anyone who pulled this trigger, because I don't want anyone to come after me." Then I awoke.

It was about 3 or 4 am, and in the quiet of that early morning, the Lord told me three things about that dream. First, He told me, "You never thought about Me in your dream." Of course, that was correct. Second, He asked, "Why did you wait until the end of the night to execute bin Laden? It was in your power to do it at the beginning." Finally, He said, "Because bin Laden sat in your presence, then you could not enjoy your family and friends." I really cannot tell you how many times worry and anxiety have robbed me of joy in my life. And in my dream, among family and friends who I enjoy the most, I could not enjoy it.

Then the Lord said, "Here is how I am going to teach you to overcome worry and anxiety: Focus on me. Consider worry and anxiety as enemies of your life. You will deal with them at the beginning of each day and learn to enjoy the people in your life."

I have changed my mind about worry and anxiety. They are neither normal nor inevitable. They are common, but they are not normal. Jesus is normal, while nothing else is. We often worry because we expect and accept it as normal. It robs us of our families and our joy. It distracts us from God. Worry and anxiety exist because we

allow them to, but we do not have to do so. With
God, we are in control of our lives. He would
not ask us to do something if we didn't have the
ability to do it. So when God says, "Do not worry.
Do not be anxious," He gives us the power to do it.

Chapter Ten

3 Ways to Overcome Worry and Anxiety

I want to give you three ways to overcome worry and anxiety:

1. Consider Worry and Anxiety as Enemies

Worry and anxiety are your adversaries. What was the significance of my dream about Osama bin Laden? The enemy was present, but he was not active; he just sat there with no intention or ability to hurt or kill me. The devil throws all kinds of things into your life that just sit there and intimidate you. Like in my dream, worry and anxiety rob you of your ability to worship, fellowship, and love people.

Attack the bin Ladens in your life every morning. Don't let them sit there and rob you. You may have a financial bin Laden, a relationship bin Laden, or a health bin Laden. Destroy them every morning. They will be unable to rob you of your enjoyment throughout the day.

2. Turn Thoughts into Prayers

Turn every anxious and worrisome thought into a prayer until you have victory. Remember Paul's words to the Philippians:

> Be anxious for nothing, but in everything by prayer and supplication, with thanksgiving, let your requests be made known to God; and the peace of God, which surpasses all understanding, will guard your hearts and minds through Christ Jesus (Philippians 4:6–7).

Every morning when you awake, in addition to your prayer list, have a worry list—a list that says, "This is what is bothering me today." Many times, when you are trying to pray, your mind may wander. Do you know where it usually travels? To those things that bother you. You may have a meeting today with a boss you don't like. Perhaps you have a test to take this afternoon. You might have a money problem. So make your worry list part of your new prayer list.

Paul wanted the Philippians to make their requests known to God with thanksgiving. That means that we should thank Him that He loves us, hears us, and will answer our prayers. Say, "Thank you Father that You love me, You care for me, You know everything that is happening in my life, and You will hear and answer me." The devil wants you to think that you are on your own and that you have to solve your own problems. He is a liar! You have a loving Daddy who wants to help you with every circumstance. If you are sitting around worrying, you are wasting that relationship.

Nothing could give you more comfort. If Bill Gates was your father, you would probably think that you would never have to worry about anything ever again, right? Well, your Daddy can buy Bill Gates a billion times over and not exhaust the change in one pocket!

When you have prayed through your worry and anxiety, the Bible says that you will have peace. I can remember older saints who talked about "praying through" an issue. They meant that they would pray until they got that peace, which will guard your mind and heart. The Greek word translated *guard* here is *Phrourēsei*, which means to guard against a military invasion. Thank God for everything. He will set a military guard around your heart so that the devil cannot penetrate it with worry and anxiety. Make your prayers practical. What is coming against you? Grab hold of your Daddy's hand and attack it. Kill the bin Ladens in your life first thing in the morning so that they are not bothering you all day long. Don't let them ruin your party or your relationships.

3. Believe in Faith and Confess God's Love

Finally, believe by faith and confess that God is your loving Daddy and that He cares for you. Remember what Jesus said:

> "Therefore do not worry, saying, 'What shall we eat?' or 'What shall we drink?' or 'What shall we wear?' For after all these things the Gentiles seek. For your heavenly Father knows that you need all these things. But seek first the kingdom of God and His righteousness, and all these things shall be added to you" (Matthew 6:31–33).

Do not worry. Do not be anxious. You have the best Daddy in the world, and He is your answer to every worry and anxiety.

Part 4

I Changed My Mind About Insecurity

Chapter Eleven

3 Worldly Causes of Insecurity

Insecurity is a lack of confidence on a personal level and an uncertainty or anxiety about yourself. You can experience insecurity in many different ways. For example, you might experience global insecurity, or insecurity about all or most of life's circumstances. Later, I will share my wife Karen's experience. At the time of this writing, we have been married over 40 years, but when I met Karen, she expressed more insecurity than any person I had ever met. She struggled with self-hatred and self-image problems. You will see how God transformed her life and freed her from those insecurities.

You may also have situational insecurity. I always felt that I was a confident person, although I did have some areas of insecurity. If you had walked up to Karen 40 years ago and she found you intimidating, then she would have cowered and shied away from you. If you had approached me and I felt insecure, then I would have stuck out my chest, stood my ground, and stared at you. I would act confident on the outside so that I could cover for my insecurity on the inside.

I believe that every person deals with some issues related to insecurity. We simply have different ways of dealing with them. Some may turn to God while others turn away. Some may turn to addictive substances. However, all of us will deal with those issues in some way, either right or wrong. When you deal with it, it is an opportunity for either God or the devil to work in your life. You may become insecure, falsely secure, or secure in Christ. The only true remedy for insecurity is a personal relationship with Jesus Christ. You will see Jesus as the same cure for issues throughout this entire book.

THE ONLY TRUE REMEDY
FOR INSECURITY IS A
PERSONAL RELATIONSHIP
WITH JESUS CHRIST.

1. Money

What is one of the most popular ways that the world finds security? Money, right? In fact, there are financial instruments called *securities*. In 2008, however, we learned that they are not so *secure*. I grew up in the Texas Panhandle region. One couple we knew had made an enormous fortune from the oil and gas industry. They had a net worth of hundreds of millions of dollars, yet they were generous, philanthropic people. They owned several homes in different places around the world as well as an apartment in New York City. One day, home intruders robbed the wife at knifepoint in the apartment. The intruders stole jewelry, artwork, and other possessions. After the incident, the wife sat down beside one of our pastors. She said, "I live in constant fear every day that I am going to get killed for my money." She had more money than she could ever need, but she was still insecure.

Money can be a good thing, but if you believe that money itself can make you secure, then you are deceived. Jesus spoke about the "deceit-fulness of riches" (Matthew 13:22; Mark 4:19). Money is important and a blessing, but God is essential. Money can bring some security, but only Christ can make you truly secure. The apostle Paul told the Philippians,

> I have learned in whatever state I am, to be content .... Everywhere and in all things I have learned both to be full and to be hungry, both to abound and to suffer need (Philippians 4:11–12).

Paul was saying that he could be secure regard-less of how much money he had. When Jesus Christ is in our lives, we can be secure.

2. Appearance

The world also finds security in looks, in appearance. If you are not careful, even as a believer, you may do the same thing. It is no sin to want to look your best. However, I am now in my sixties, and my body has changed. I have learned that gravity will always win in the end! My grandkids always want to go the swimming pool in the summer. I used to put on some self-tanning lotion to give me little more confidence. But now, I have decided that my job at the swimming pool is to make other people feel better about their bodies. It has become a ministry!

Fashion models, in spite of their beauty, can suffer from very low self-esteem. The reason for this is that they are always comparing themselves to each other. It is a brutal industry and often exploitative in the way it treats women. My wife is more beautiful than any of those airbrushed models. The more babies she's had and the older she gets, the more beautiful she has become. Beauty is not only in appearance.

3. "Comparing Up"

A big part of what causes insecurity in the world is "comparing up," which I wrote about earlier. Some people drive into a parking lot and immediately notice the cars that are nicer than theirs are. Many people find that experience tormenting. Instead, I recommend occasionally comparing down. I mean, make yourself aware of the worst looking cars, and then give God thanks. Better yet, don't compare at all!

Chapter Twelve

Psalm 91: The Antidote for Insecurity

As believers, we should think differently than the world thinks, even though the world's thinking does affect all of us to some degree. The Bible has answers to this problem. Some Scripture passages specifically address it. For example, 1 Corinthians 13 is the love chapter, Hebrews 11 is the faith chapter, and Psalm 91 is the security chapter.

> He who dwells in the secret place of the
> Most High
> Shall abide under the shadow of the
> Almighty.
> I will say of the Lord, *"He is* my refuge
> and my fortress;
> My God, in Him I will trust"
> (Psalm 91:1–2).

In the first line, the psalmist[7] writes about the *secret place*. Where is the secret place where we will live under the shelter of God? Jesus said,

> "But you, when you pray, go into your room, and when you have shut your door, pray to your Father who *is* in the secret *place;* and your Father who sees in secret will reward you openly" (Matthew 6:6).

Go into your personal space and pray. The God who sees you in that secret place will reward you openly.

In verse 2, the psalmist says that the Lord is our refuge and fortress and we should trust in Him. This confession is from a person who lives a secure life. If you go into your secret place and are feeling insecure about your finances, looks, or relationships, then where will you turn? Where you turn will be your security. You should turn to God. I will not put my trust and security in relationships, money, or people. *"God, You are*

---

[7] The authorship of this psalm is uncertain. Most biblical scholars ascribe it to either David or Moses.

the only One who can give me real security." I am going to say that with my mouth—it is my confession. It comes from my personal relationship with God.

The psalmist continues with some marvelous promises:

> Surely He shall deliver you from the
>   snare of the fowler
> *And* from the perilous pestilence.
> He shall cover you with His feathers,
> And under His wings you shall take
>   refuge;
> His truth *shall be your* shield and buckler.
> You shall not be afraid of the terror by
>   night,
> *Nor* of the arrow *that* flies by day,
> *Nor* of the pestilence *that* walks in
>   darkness,
> *Nor* of the destruction *that* lays waste at
>   noonday.
> A thousand may fall at your side,
> And ten thousand at your right hand;
> *But* it shall not come near you.
> Only with your eyes shall you look,
> And see the reward of the wicked.

Because you have made the Lord, *who is*
my refuge,
Even the Most High, your dwelling place,
No evil shall befall you,
Nor shall any plague come near your
dwelling;
For He shall give His angels charge over
you,
To keep you in all your ways.
In *their* hands they shall bear you up,
Lest you dash your foot against a stone.
You shall tread upon the lion and the
cobra,
The young lion and the serpent you shall
trample underfoot (Psalm 91:3–13).

This confession comes from a secure individual! God says,

I will be with you. I will protect you and deliver you from everything that might harm you. You will trample down the serpent and the lion. You will not live your life in fear and insecurity. You will be a confident warrior for Me. It doesn't matter how much money you have, how young or old you are, how you look, or how popular you are.

Thank God that it begins and ends with Him.

Because he has set his love upon Me,
    therefore I will deliver him;
I will set him on high, because he has
    known My name.
He shall call upon Me, and I will answer
    him;
I *will be* with him in trouble;
I will deliver him and honor him
With long life I will satisfy him,
And show him My salvation
    (Psalm 91:14–16).

"I will show him My salvation." Is that not an awesome promise? That is God's promise to you, if you will turn to Him in prayer and believe in Him for your life and security.

Chapter Thirteen

A Spirit of King Saul or the Apostle Paul?

I mentioned earlier that when we got married, Karen expressed a lot of insecurity. She was a believer, but it was still hard for her to believe God loved her. She wanted to know God, but she hated herself.

When we married, she made a commitment to read the Bible every day. Keep this verse in mind and write it down—you will want to come back to it:

> He sent His word and healed them, And delivered *them* from their destructions (Psalm 107:20).

At first, when she read the Bible, Karen didn't believe the loving parts of it. She believed

Leviticus—the law and judgment chapters. For forty years now, she has read the Bible first thing every day. But you don't just read the Bible—*the Bible reads you*. The author of Hebrews says,

> The Word of God *is* living and powerful, and sharper than any two-edged sword (Hebrews 4:12).

One edge of the sword is a scalpel that heals us; the other edge is a blade that slays the enemies of God.

We can also compare the Bible to software that God originally designed our hardware (bodies) to run on. When you read the Bible, it reprograms your hardware, so that you can live successfully. Psalm 1 says that if you meditate on the Bible, you will succeed in everything you do. God's Word reprograms you and even has a sin virus-killing program in it!

Karen had a severe problem with low self-esteem. She would often stand behind me in public because she was extremely shy. Even at home, I must confess that I would dominate her as well. Every time there was a problem, I would convince her it was her problem. However, as she began to read the Bible over a couple of years, she gained the confidence to stand up to me. I am ashamed to say that I didn't respond very well.

During that time, I constantly played golf. One day, I came home, and Karen really stood up to me for the first time. I tried to get her to sit down so that I could explain that her complaint was her problem and her fault. Again, I'm embarrassed to say that I was being a verbal bully. When she didn't accept my version of the situation, I responded by telling her to get out of the house and go back to her parents. She wouldn't back down. Now I can say, Praise the Lord! That was the night that God broke through my heart and began to heal our marriage. Today, my wife is a lioness for God. I certainly cannot take any credit for it. God healed her and transformed her by His Word—and He straightened me out as well!

Nobody can read the Bible for you. The devil wants it to sit on your shelf and gather dust.

Before he tries to defeat you, he must disarm you. The Bible is the sword of the Spirit—pick up your sword and you can defeat any enemy. Today my wife is a loving, confident person through the power of the Spirit and the weapon of the Word.

7 Signs of a King Saul Spirit

The story of King Saul is recorded in 1 and 2 Samuel. Before Saul, God was Israel's king. Other nations surrounding Israel had human monarchs, but Israel did not. The Israelites demanded a king so that they could be like the other nations. I suspect that God probably felt something like this:

Well, I am sorry you feel that way. I think that I have been a very good king and been doing a pretty good job. But if you really want a human king, then I will give you one. Just be ready—because he is going to break your heart.

God told them exactly what would happen if they had a human king, but since they insisted,

THE BIBLE IS THE SWORD
OF THE SPIRIT—PICK UP
YOUR SWORD AND YOU CAN
DEFEAT ANY ENEMY.

He gave them Saul as the first king of Israel. And Saul was a totally insecure man. Rather than turn his insecurities over to God, Saul let the enemy take charge. He did just about everything wrong, to the point where God regretted making him king. Eventually, when God rejected Saul, Samuel anointed David as king. David was "a man after God's own heart" (1 Samuel 13:14; Acts 13:22).

These are the 7 signs or characteristics of a King Saul spirit:

1. UNTEACHABLE AND UNAPPROACHABLE

King Saul was unteachable and unapproachable. If you are insecure, then no one can tell you anything. Saul gave all who came to him that kind of treatment—he rejected them and refused to listen to what they had to say.

2. JEALOUS AND ENVIOUS

King Saul was full of jealousy and envy. When David killed Goliath, the people of Israel began to sing a song about how Saul had killed his thousands, but David his tens of thousands (1 Samuel 29:5). Saul became so envious of David that he tried to kill him (1 Samuel 19). This applies especially to some of us as parents. Do you remember the Wanda Holloway cheerleader story that I told earlier? I have seen many parents and coaches who scream at young athletes during sporting events. If you are so fragile and insecure that you must win at everything, then something is wrong. I have played golf with some people like that. Don't respond that way to competition. Keep your dignity and character at all times.

3. PASSING BLAME

King Saul transferred blame to others. He did not destroy the Amalekites completely as God had commanded him to do. When he returned and Samuel reproached him for his disobedience, Saul blamed the people (1 Samuel 15:15).

4. NEEDING TO CONTROL

King Saul needed to control, and he tried to destroy anything that he could not. He had a controlling spirit—much in the way I did when I married Karen.

5. ANGRY AND EMOTIONALLY UNSTABLE

Anger and emotional instability ruled King Saul. He suffered from demon-inspired fits of rage to the point that he would try to kill David. Saul once tried to pin him against a wall with a spear (1 Samuel 18:11). We all feel anger, but when it controls our lives, then it becomes an opportunity for the devil.

6. UNBELIEVING AND SPIRITUALLY COMPROMISING

King Saul gave in to unbelief and spiritual compromise. He once sought out a witch for counsel (1 Samuel 28:3–25). He was trying to find a place of security apart from God.

King Saul feared others. When he did not obey God regarding the Amalekites, he said he feared the people (1 Samuel 15:24). He cared what the people would think. All of us care somewhat about what others think of us. However, Jesus told His followers to beware when people speak well of us (Luke 6:26). Such praise may be false, and it doesn't matter what others think of us. It matters what God thinks of us.

Saul was such a completely insecure man that he turned inward instead of to God. And the results were disastrous.

3 Steps to an Apostle Paul Spirit

There was another Saul in the Bible ... you may know him as the apostle Paul. He said,

And lest I should be exalted above measure by the abundance of the revelations, a thorn in the flesh was given to me, a messenger of Satan to buffet me, lest I be exalted above measure. Concerning this thing I pleaded with the Lord three times that it might depart from me. And He said to me, "My grace is sufficient for you, for My strength is made perfect in weakness." Therefore most gladly I will rather boast in my infirmities, that the power of Christ may rest upon me. Therefore I take pleasure in infirmities, in reproaches, in needs, in persecutions, in distresses, for Christ's sake. For when I am weak, then I am strong (2 Corinthians 12:7–10).

The apostle Paul's spirit is the opposite of the King Saul spirit. In this Scripture, Paul explains that he was given a thorn in the flesh, or a physical affliction. Remember that God either causes or allows everything that happens to us. He allowed Paul to have this thorn. No one knows for sure what it was, though some Bible scholars note that Paul seemed to have an eye problem when he wrote to the Galatians. Nevertheless, he hated it no matter what it was. Paul asked God three times to take it away, but God explained that His grace was sufficient for Paul. God's power would be made perfect in Paul's weakness.

There are 3 steps to an apostle Paul spirit for dealing with insecurity.

1. TURN TO GOD

First, turn to God, as Paul did. The Lord is your security in every time of trouble. Go to your secret place and lay your burdens before Him in prayer.

2. EMBRACE YOUR WEAKNESS

The apostle Paul embraced his weakness. I am not saying to never try improving your situation. You don't have to accept everything that comes into your life. Remember, however, what Viktor Frankl said about changing your attitude when you cannot change the situation.

If you had a magic wand that you could wave over your life and body, and you could change anything that you want to change—would it be worth it? Would you want to pick it up, wave it, and become healthy, wealthy, and powerful? God forbid! The things that make us feel bad and those that cause us pain make us aware of our need for God. The things that we endure make us stronger. Again, look at what Paul says:

> And not only *that,* but we also glory in tribulations, knowing that tribulation produces perseverance; and perseverance, character; and character, hope (Romans 5:3–4).

Our glory in tribulation results in giving us hope. Hope is one of the three great characteristics of the godly, along with faith and love. Hope, then, is another way to define security. We have security in God because of the hope of the promises He gives to us.

God loves being our Daddy. We are weak like sheep, and we need a Savior and a Shepherd. You may try, like those who live in the world, to run from your weakness by taking some substance or engaging in behavior that provides temporary pleasure or relief. Don't do it! It does not work. The difference between the way the world thinks and the way we think is this: the world runs to something, but we run to Someone.

THE DIFFERENCE BETWEEN
THE WAY THE WORLD THINKS
AND THE WAY WE THINK IS
THIS: THE WORLD RUNS TO
SOMETHING, BUT WE RUN
TO SOMEONE.

His power put together with your weakness makes you and God a perfect team! When you admit that you need Him, He will be there. That confession leads to strength and hope, which provide security. But you will not find God until you admit your need for Him.

3. PUT YOUR FAITH IN GOD'S GRACE

The final step is to put your faith in God's grace. You don't have to do anything to deserve it, because you don't deserve anything. Grace is God's unmerited favor, which is why He told Paul that His grace is sufficient. God's grace opens up His lap for you to jump in. His lap is a place of unconditional love, grace, and joy. It is open to you no matter how badly you have messed up in the past.

At the conclusion, Paul says that he rejoices in everything in his life about which he would ordinarily feel insecure. Paul reminds us how badly we need the Lord and that when we go to Him, we can be secure.

Part 5
I Changed My Mind About Fear

Chapter Fourteen

Why Did Jesus Experience Fear?

How should we think about fear? Next to the command to love, the commandment "Do not fear" is one of the most used in the Bible. God does not want us to live in fear. He did not create us to fear; He created us to live in peace. When God made Adam and Eve in the garden of Eden, there was peace; it was a paradise. Jesus is the Prince of Peace, but the devil brings fear into our lives, just as he brought it into the garden in the first place.

Luke recounts the events of Jesus in the garden of Gethsemane, the night before Jesus' death:

Coming out, He went to the Mount of Olives, as He was accustomed, and His disciples also followed

GOD DOES NOT WANT
US TO LIVE IN FEAR. HE
DID NOT CREATE US TO
FEAR; HE CREATED US
TO LIVE IN PEACE.

Him. When He came to the place, He said to them, "Pray that you may not enter into temptation."

And He was withdrawn from them about a stone's throw, and He knelt down and prayed, saying, "Father, if it is Your will, take this cup away from Me; nevertheless not My will, but Yours, be done." Then an angel appeared to Him from heaven, strengthening Him. And being in agony, He prayed more earnestly. Then His sweat became like great drops of blood falling down to the ground.

When He rose up from prayer, and had come to His disciples, He found them sleeping from sorrow. Then He said to them, "Why do you sleep? Rise and pray, lest you enter into temptation."

And while He was still speaking, behold, a multitude; and he who was called Judas, one of the twelve, went before them and drew near to Jesus to kiss Him (Luke 22:39–47).

Clearly, Jesus was in agony—the Greek word *agonia* means great fear or distress. Jesus felt more fear in that moment than any human being has ever felt. Luke also says that Jesus' sweat became like great drops of blood. The medical term for this condition is *hematohidrosis,* which is a rare condition in which small blood vessels leading to the sweat glands rupture under conditions of intense stress. Jesus actually sweated blood.

Jesus experienced real fear, but He also defeated it. And because He defeated it, we can do the same. Jesus actually shows us how to do it. Several times, He could have experienced fear before Gethsemane. So why did Jesus experience fear in the garden? Why did He experience fear at all?

Jesus Identified with Us

The first reason that Jesus felt fear is so that He could identify with us as human beings. Remember, Jesus is fully God, but He is also fully man. Our Savior has a human mother named Mary. Jesus was born into this world like any other baby. He grew up in the village of Nazareth in a less-than-perfect human family. As a human, Jesus can identify with us:

Seeing then that we have a great High Priest who has passed through the heavens, Jesus the Son of God, let us hold fast *our* confession. For we do not have a High Priest who cannot sympathize with our weaknesses, but was in all *points* tempted as *we are, yet* without sin. Let us therefore come boldly to the throne of grace, that we may obtain mercy and find grace to help in time of need. For every high priest taken from among men is appointed for men in things *pertaining* to God, that he may offer both gifts and sacrifices for sins. He can have compassion on those who are ignorant and going astray, since he himself is also subject to weakness (Hebrews 4:14–5:2).

Yes, Jesus was tempted in every way that we are, yet He was without sin. What tempted Him in the garden of Gethsemane? Did He want to run away? When Jesus entered the garden, He instructed His disciples,

"Pray that you may not enter into temptation" (Matthew 26:41).

He must have been hinting to them about what was soon to come. Perhaps Jesus was showing extra concern for them during what would be an especially stressful and traumatic event.

Satan wants to fill you with fear so that you will not do God's will. Every time you make a decision based on fear, you do not make one based on God's will. You will regret every fear-based decision you make. God's will was for Jesus to go to the cross. Three times Jesus prayed and told the Father that He really didn't want to do this. But in the end, He told the Father,

"Not My will, but Your will be done" (Luke 22:42).

Thank God that our Savior acted above His fears. As disciples, we should follow His example and act above our fears. Fear will always be present to some degree, but we have a High Priest who understands every circumstance that we face and a loving Father who promised to bring us to victory by His Holy Spirit.

Always hold on to God's love and grace. The devil is trying to convince you that God is a mean, austere, and troubled deity—that He is already angry with you. The enemy wants you to think that God only sees all the dumb and sinful stuff you have done, and God doesn't really want you to be close to Him. The devil tries to deceive you into believing that maybe God wants you in His family, but He really wants you to stand away from Him at a distance. Nothing could be further from the truth! Our high priest is madly in love with His children. Jesus calls you *His friend*!

Jesus said,

> "I am gentle and lowly in heart, and you will find rest for your souls" (Matthew 11:29).

Our Lord Jesus is a marvelous God. He understands and has experienced every fear and every temptation that we have. He knows exactly how we feel. Jesus felt fear in the garden so that He could identify with us, and we could identify with Him.

Jesus Knew He Would Face the Cross

Jesus also felt fear at Gethsemane because He had full knowledge of what He was about experience on the cross. We often feel fear because of what we do not know. What will happen tomorrow? What will happen with your job, your children, or your health? We don't know, so we give in to worry and insecurity. But Jesus knew. He knew what was about to happen. Jesus died the most painful and grisly death imaginable, but He knew every single detail of what was to come.

Jesus had raised a man from the dead with only two words: "Lazarus, arise" (John 11:43). As the Son of God, Jesus didn't have to pray twice about anything. Still, at Gethsemane, He went before the Father three times and asked, "Please take Me out of this if there is any way. I don't want to drink this cup ... not My will, but Your will be done." Immediately, an angel came and strengthened Jesus after He made this declaration. Luke says that He then prayed even *more* earnestly. Only then did Jesus sweat blood. The tension had

JESUS DIED THE MOST
PAINFUL AND GRISLY
DEATH IMAGINABLE,
BUT HE KNEW EVERY
SINGLE DETAIL OF
WHAT WAS TO COME.

reached its highest point, His stress its highest level. The agony of the crucifixion was now inevitable. Jesus knew everything that He was about to suffer, and He did it for our sake.

The Enemy Launched a Full-Scale Assault

Another reason that Jesus was fearful was because Satan, the real spirit of fear, launched a full-scale assault against Him. Fear is not something—it is someone. The fourth chapter of Luke records that Jesus fasted for 40 days before Satan confronted Him. Luke wrote about the end of that attack in the wilderness:

"Now when the devil had ended every temptation, he departed from Him until an opportune time" (Luke 4:13).

You must know this about the nature of the devil: He is an opportunist. When you are the weakest and most vulnerable, he is the most

FEAR IS
NOT SOMETHING—
IT IS SOMEONE.

evil. Generally, when you know that someone is hurting, you will let up or be gentle with them. Your enemy operates in the opposite way. When you are hurting, he presses in and tries to do his worst.

Satan failed his opportunity in the wilderness, so he looked for another chance. He thought he had it in the garden of Gethsemane. Jesus was weak and troubled there. Satan thought it was an opportune time, so he came with his spirit of fear. The apostle Paul says,

> For God has not given us a spirit of fear, but of power and of love and of a sound mind (2 Timothy 1:7).

The devil does not control your thoughts, but he does influence them. He whispers thoughts of fear to you, hoping that you will accept them so that he can control your life. God will never use fear to control your life.

GOD WILL NEVER
USE FEAR TO
CONTROL YOUR LIFE.

Chapter Fifteen

Good Fear versus Bad Fear

When the Bible refers to the *fear of the Lord*, it means a reverence for God. It is a positive emotion, not a negative one.

The author of Hebrews says,

> Inasmuch then as the children have partaken of flesh and blood, He Himself likewise shared in the same, that through death He might destroy him who had the power of death, that is, the devil, and release those who through fear of death were all their lifetime subject to bondage (Hebrews 2:14–15).

Ultimately, all fear is the fear of death. You may say that you have a fear of snakes. No, you really have a fear of dying from a snake bite! Do you have a fear of heights? No, you have a fear of falling from up high to your death. Claustrophobia? You have a fear of suffocation. If you think it through carefully, all fears come from the fear of death. We fear that which can harm us, or at least that which we think can harm us, and the ultimate harm is death.

Here, however, is the good news: You will never die! The fear of death is a lie. Satan holds people in bondage through the fear of death. But Jesus told Martha,

> "I am the resurrection and the life. He who believes in Me, though he may die, he shall live. And whoever lives and believes in Me shall never die. Do you believe this?" (John 11:25–26).

You will never, in all eternity, experience a moment of death. Your spirit is eternal; it will never be buried in a casket in the ground. Your body will die, but God will one day reunite it with your spirit. The instant that your eyes close on earth, they will open in heaven. Jesus told the thief on the cross,

"Assuredly, I say to you, today you will be with Me in paradise" (Luke 23:43).

Joseph of Arimathea had Jesus' body placed in an earthly tomb, but Jesus' Spirit went straight to the right hand of the Father. And the same is true for you. The moment you go numb here, your senses will come alive there. The instant you take your last breath here, you take your first breath there.

You will never die. So when the devil tries to put the fear of death in you, understand that it is just a demonic spirit from hell trying to give you a negative view of the future. It wants you to make a fear-based decision, one which God will not honor. Faith comes from the Spirit of God. It gives you a positive view of the future, so that you will make a faith-based decision that God will honor. Faith gives you hope, and hope does not let you down (Romans 5:5).

The Differences Between Good and Bad Fear

God wants you to test and distinguish between different types of spirits (1 John 4:1). The same instruction can be made about fear. You need to be able to discern between good and bad fear. The fear that we have been talking about is demonic, paralyzing fear. However, there is also good fear, such as the fear you feel when someone swerves into your lane when you are driving. That is a warning.

Good fear has 4 characteristics:

1. CIRCUMSTANTIAL VERSUS PERPETUAL

Good fear is circumstantial. You only feel the fear when the driver comes into your lane. When they pass, you are over it. Bad fear is perpetual. It hangs over you, and you constantly expect the next bad thing to happen.

2. PROTECTIVE VERSUS PARALYZING

Good fear is protective. When someone swerves into your lane, you move out of the way. Bad fear is paralyzing. You cannot find a useful response.

3. CONSTRUCTIVE VERSUS CONFUSING

Good fear is constructive. When you are under the influence of good fear, you can do the right thing. Bad fear is confusing and fatalistic. It clouds your reasoning.

4. EMPOWERING VERSUS ENSLAVING

Good fear is empowering. You have likely heard stories about ordinary people who do seemingly impossible things in difficult situations, such as someone lifting a car off another person pinned underneath. The flow of adrenaline enables that person to perform an almost superhuman act. The Holy Spirit is like spiritual adrenaline that gives believers power that isn't natural—it's supernatural.

On the other hand, bad fear is enslaving. Once, on a long commercial flight, I sat across the aisle from a young woman who was flying for the first time. She was terrified. Her friends attempted to console her, but she started using the airsick bag even before we left the gate. She remained nauseated throughout the flight. I thought to myself, how horrible it is to have that kind of fear. The enemy of our souls will do everything possible to turn the children of God into slaves of fear.

Chapter Sixteen

3 Steps to Overcoming Fear

You can only give away what you have. The devil has fear, and that is all he has. So fear is born of the devil, but peace comes from God.

Peace is the opposite of fear. The prophet Isaiah says there is no peace for the wicked (Isaiah 48:22). It follows that the devil has no peace. When you rebel against God, there is no way to find peace. You may try to find solace in another source, like a pill or a bottle, but you cannot get peace from those things. Peace is God's property, while fear is the province of the devil. As much as you know the presence of God by peace, you know the presence of the devil by fear. When you change your mind about fear, you will be able to recognize the difference.

Please understand that having fear does not mean that you are demon-possessed. It simply means the devil is trying to influence you to get you to do the wrong thing. This is the point at which you need faith. Fear is expecting the devil to move, while faith is expecting God to move—you make the choice. Do you remember what I wrote earlier about attitude? You choose your attitude. You can choose to put your eyes on the devil or on God. When you put your eyes upon God, you will see the example of Jesus. He rules by peace, because He has overcome fear and death.

Would you like to overcome fear the same way that Jesus did? You can if you follow these steps.

1. Admit Your Fear

First, admit your fear without shame. You don't have to be ashamed—we all feel fear. Jesus felt fear in the garden of Gethsemane. You don't have to hide it; God wants things out in the open. The devil is a creature of darkness. You cannot deal with fear until you bring it out into the light.

Jesus said, "Father, I feel the fear. I don't want to do this." The truth will literally make you free. When you expose fear for the enemy that it is—not something natural but something supernatural from the devil—then the Holy Spirit can help you deal with it.

2. Submit Your Fears to God

The second thing that you should do to overcome fear is submit it to God. You can go to God and say, "Lord, I am feeling this fear right now." As Franklin Roosevelt said, "The only thing you have to fear is fear itself." And Mark Twain said, "Courage is not the absence of fear, but the mastery of it."

Soldiers who fought and died for our nation felt fear, but they acted above their fears. Similarly, mature believers act above their emotions. Many times, you will feel angry and have to act above it. Sometimes you will feel a desire for revenge or face sexual temptation, but you must act above those as well. Emotions and fears are real, but it does not mean they are right. You have to act above them. When Jesus went to the Father, He acted above His emotions. He said, "Not My will, but Your will be done." When He said this, an angel came to strengthen Him. Praise God—if He will send the Spirit to aid Jesus in the garden, then He will come to your rescue as well.

The worst time to make a decision is when you are feeling fear. It is then that you need outside counsel. You need someone else, someone with a broader perspective and more experience, to help you discern or to tell you what to do. Not only do you need other believers, but the best counsel is the Spirit of God! He has the perspective to help you make good decisions and to discern right from wrong.

As I said earlier, I am an avid golfer. One of the greatest golfers of all time is Ben Hogan. He was always so calm and dignified on the golf course. During an interview one time late in his career, a reporter asked him how he stayed so calm. Ben responded, "I am not calm. I am terrified. I am constantly terrified on the golf course. The reason I gave up golf is that I got tired of getting sick every time a golf tournament came up. I was in constant fear." Great people, including great athletes, feel fear. Nevertheless, great people act above it.

3. Focus on God's Presence and Love

Finally, to overcome fear, focus on God's presence and love. When the children of Israel came to edge of the Promised Land, they knew giants lived there. Of the 12 spies sent into the land, 10 came out and said, "We are like grasshoppers in our own sight. Those people are huge, and they will destroy us if we go there" (Numbers 13:33). However, Joshua and Caleb said that God would give His people Canaan, and the people there would be like Israel's prey: "Let us go up at once and take possession, for we are well able to overcome it" (Numbers 13:30).

How do you see things? It is in your perspective and attitude. Ten spies came out, and their bad report terrified the nation of Israel. But two spies came out and said, "We see a big God and a little devil. Let's go in and take the land." They focused on the presence of God. They had a godly attitude. How big is your devil? Even more, how big is your God? Remember, the Lord is omnipresent; the devil is not. The universe cannot contain our God. Satan is just a created being.

David said,

> Yea, though I walk through the valley of the shadow of death, I will fear no evil; For You are with me; Your rod and Your staff, they comfort me (Psalm 23:4).

When David references "the shadow of death," he is not writing about the shadow of a hangnail or the shadow of a headache. It is the shadow of death. And David says, "I do not fear because you are with me." David focuses on God's presence. Jesus did the same on His way to the cross, even as the devil was trying to terrify Him.

> I have set the Lord always before me;
> Because *He is* at my right hand I shall not
>   be moved.
> Therefore my heart is glad, and my glory
>   rejoices;
> My flesh also will rest in hope.
> For You will not leave my soul in Sheol,
> Nor will You allow Your Holy One to see
>   corruption.
> You will show me the path of life;
> In Your presence *is* fullness of joy;
> At Your right hand *are* pleasures
>   forevermore (Psalm 16:8–11).

Jesus rejoiced because of God's presence. On the way to the cross, Satan was telling Jesus that He had disappointed His Father, and that He was a huge failure: "You are going to die on that cross and rot in hell because God will not save you."

Jesus knew that His Father would not leave Him in Sheol (the place of death). God would not allow His Holy One to see corruption. In His presence, there was fullness of joy. Jesus knew that God would always be present with Him. Likewise, the Lord is always present with you. Oh, Father, let us be more aware of You! Fear is reality minus God; faith is reality plus God. If you could fully open your eyes to the spiritual realm, you would never fear again.

When I first began to preach, little kids would sit, listen, and draw pictures of me. Their parents would bring the drawings to me after the worship service. Admittedly, some of their artwork was not very flattering, and I had to forgive them! But I remember those pictures to this day. Interestingly, different children at different times drew me preaching with two huge angels next to me. It happened once and then again a few months later. A year later, another came, and then two years later, yet another. I think that these little children could see something in the Spirit that adults often cannot see.

The author of Hebrews says that angels are ministering spirits sent to render aid to God's people (Hebrews 1:14). An angel ministered to Jesus in the garden of Gethsemane. There are angels all around you. They are with you in your home and at your workplace. They are with you at the hospital when you are very ill. Even more, God is here. His Holy Spirit abides in you and all around you. You cannot see these spirits with your physical eyes. But, as a believer, you have the ability to make the choice to have spiritual eyes that walk by faith and not by sight. You have the ability to choose an attitude of faith. When you walk by faith with the Lord before you, you cannot be moved.

I want you to change your mind about fear. Stop accepting it as a normal part of your life. Choose instead the attitude of faith. Choose the attitude of Joshua and Caleb on the edge of Canaan. Choose the attitude of Jesus in the garden of Gethsemane. Then you will know the truth—and the truth will set you free.

Conclusion

The Importance of Change: Finishing Well

You have surely heard the maxim "It's not how you start, but how you finish." One of Jesus' parables provides a powerful example of this simple truth:

"There was a man who had two sons. He went to the first and said, 'Son, go and work today in the vineyard.'

"'I will not,' he answered, but later he **changed his mind** and went.

"Then the father went to the other son and said the same thing. He answered, 'I will, sir,' but he did not go.

"Which of the two did what his father wanted?"

"The first," they answered.

Jesus said to them, "Truly I tell you, the tax collectors and the prostitutes are entering the kingdom of God ahead of you. For John came to you to show you the way of righteousness, and you did not believe him, but the tax collectors and the prostitutes did. And even after you saw this, you did not repent and believe him" (Matthew 21:28–32 NIV emphasis added).

Change happens, and, as we have seen, we all have a choice of how and what we will change. As Paul said in Romans, we are changed—transformed—by the renewal of our minds.

God wants to transform our minds, not only so that we think differently but also as a means of transforming our behavior, for we are created to do good works (Ephesians 2:10). When our minds have been *renewed*, we will understand God's perfect will for our life and move toward spiritual maturity. Putting spiritual maturity into action is what enables us, as it did Paul, to pursue our highest goal:

I press on toward the goal to win the prize for which God has called me heavenward in Christ Jesus (Philippians 3:14 NIV).

Fortunately, the race we run is a marathon. Like the two sons above, we have a choice when it comes to change.

Choosing Your Attitude

We learned earlier how important attitude is, and how we can build a good attitude by adopting these characteristics:

1. Gratitude
2. Faith
3. Humility
4. Graciousness
5. Respect
6. Servanthood
7. Contentment

In the parable above, we only see the beginning and end for those sons. However, I believe that we can say for sure that the first son's mind was renewed to embrace the seven characteristics above. Both sons chose their attitudes. God rewarded and disciplined their attitudes. Both sons' attitudes predicted and preceded their future. While we cannot know what specific issues led these sons to change their minds, we can take steps in our own lives to run the race and *finish well*.

Changing Thoughts into Actions

Transformation is a process and is different for every believer. I suggest that after choosing a positive attitude, you start by looking at just one or two things from each of the categories we discussed and commit to transform your thinking.

Success and Failure

Remember, *you* choose your standards for success and failure, and the Bible makes clear what the Lord's standards are. Think about the example of King Solomon—how well he started and how poorly he finished! What are some ways that you can strengthen your relationship with Jesus, live more focused on God, or treat others with compassion? Pray and let the Holy Spirit guide you, one step at a time, to find ways to seek a higher purpose and receive your *heavenly reward*.

Worry and Anxiety

Worry and anxiety are neither normal nor inevitable. Identify the bin Ladens in your life. What are the most bothersome worries that are robbing you of sleep at night? Attack them one by one. Turn those thoughts into prayers. When you experience trials, read James 1: 1–27. Make your requests known to God. God will give you the power to take more control of your life, so that you can overcome worry and replace it with *peace*.

Insecurity

Do you feel insecure about your finances, your appearance, or what others have? If so, take Paul's approach to this problem. Acknowledge your need for God. Turn to Him, confess your weakness, and pray for perspective. Trust in His grace. Embrace your weaknesses and remember that tribulation produces *strength* and *hope*, which provide *security*.

Fear

Jesus experienced fear just like we all do. Identify and admit your biggest fear, then submit it to God. Focus on God; He is always present with you and loves you. Remember that your attitude affects how you perceive things. Are you like Joshua and Caleb, who saw a big God and a little devil? If so, you can *rejoice* in God's presence, even as Jesus did while He was on His way to suffer on the cross.

There Is Victory

Run in such a way as to get the prize. Everyone who competes in the games goes into strict training. They do it to get a crown that will not last, but we do it to get a crown that will last forever (1 Corinthians 9:24b–25 NIV).

I pray that you will change your mind, as I changed mine, about your attitude and the obstacles that Satan places in your path. May the power of the Holy Spirit be with you so that, no matter how you may have started, you may *finish well* and receive the crown that will last forever.

About the Author

Jimmy Evans is the lead apostolic senior pastor at Gateway Church, a multi-campus church in the Dallas/Fort Worth Metroplex.

He is also the founder and CEO of MarriageToday, a ministry based in Dallas, Texas, devoted to helping couples build strong, fulfilling marriages and families. Jimmy is the host of *The Overcoming Life*, a daily television program dedicated to seeing people thrive in life and in faith.

Jimmy served as the senior pastor of Trinity Fellowship Church in Amarillo, Texas for 30 years and now serves as the senior elder. During his years of leadership, Trinity grew from 900 to over 10,000 members.

He holds an honorary doctorate of literature from The Kings University and has authored more than sixteen books including *Marriage on the Rock, Ten Steps Toward Christ, Lifelong Love Affair, When Life Hurts, The Right One*, and *Strengths Based Marriage*.

Jimmy and his wife, Karen, have been married 44 years and have two married children and five grandchildren.

TEN STEPS TOWARD CHRIST

JOURNEY TO THE HEART OF GOD

JIMMY EVANS

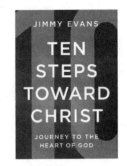

Salvation isn't the last step.
It's the first. What's next?

I've accepted Christ—now how do I live as a Christian? Practices in the church are confusing, the Bible seems overwhelming, prayer is a mystery, and I still have problems in my life. What do I do now?

With these down-to-earth principles, Jimmy Evans gives you a map to navigate your new life. He explains how to:
- Connect with God
- Relate to other Christians
- See the Bible as relevant
- Understand church customs
- Find freedom from past hurts

You can find **Ten Steps Toward Christ** at the Gateway Bookstore and wherever Chrisitan books are sold.

ISBN: 9781945529252